LITURGIES OF LAMENT

J. FRANK HENDERSON

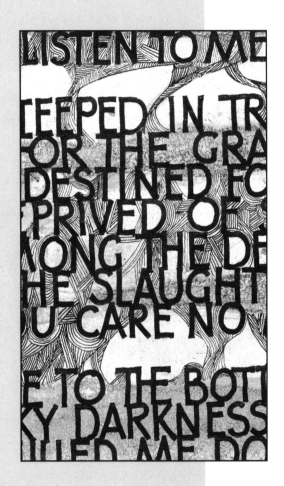

LITURGY TRAINING PUBLICATIONS

ACKNOWLEDGMENTS

This small book has a long and complex history, going back to early 1984.
Gordon Lathrop and Larry Hoffman provided stimulation and encouragement in
the initial phases of the work.

Hans Boehringer helped keep the concept alive, providing much support
and encouragement plus many fine ideas over many years. More recently, Denise
Davis Taylor provided substantial help and insight regarding lament for
violence against women.

The Christian-Jewish Dialogue of Toronto and the International Commission on
English in the Liturgy graciously allowed for texts to be included.

Many others have provided resources and opportunities to teach, write and test
ideas. The appendix on interchurch and interfaith liturgies contains revised
material originally published in the *National Bulletin on Liturgy* (May-June 1986
issue). Ruth has given me time to think and compose.

Many thanks to all of you.

Original Opening Prayers from the *Sacramentary* © 1994, International Committee
on English in the Liturgy, Inc. All rights reserved.

Copyright © 1994, Archdiocese of Chicago: Liturgy Training Publications,
1800 North Hermitage Avenue, Chicago IL 60622-1101; 1-800-933-1800;
FAX 1-800-933-7094. All rights reserved.

Liturgies of Lament was edited by David Philippart. The production editor was
Deborah Bogaert. It was designed by Jill Smith and typeset by Kari Nicholls,
and the art is by Vivian Carter. Military vehicles photo courtesy Reuters/Bettman.
Drought photo and ruins photo courtesy UPI/Bettman. Police photo by
Matt Marton. Boy and gun photo by Kip Kania. Printed
by Congress Printing Company, Chicago, Illinois.

Library of Congress Cataloging-in-Publications Data

Henderson, Frank (J. Frank)
    Liturgies of Lament / J. Frank Henderson.
      p. cm.
    Includes bibliographical references.
    ISBN 0-929650-78-6 : $11.95
      1. Occasional services. 2. Disasters — Religious aspects —
Christianity. 3. Liturgics. I. Title.
    BV199.03H37 1994   94-27599
    265'.9 — dc20   CIP

CONTENTS

88 PSALM

SAVE
ME,
LORD
MY
GOD!

SAVE ME, LORD MY GOD!
BY DAY, BY NIGHT, I CRY OUT+
LET MY PRAYER REACH YOU,
TURN, LISTEN TO ME+

I AM STEEPED IN TROUBLE,
READY FOR THE GRAVE+
I AM LIKE ONE DESTINED FOR THE PIT,
A WARRIOR DEPRIVED OF STRENGTH,
FORGOTTEN AMONG THE DEAD,
BURIED WITH THE SLAUGHTERED
FOR WHOM YOU CARE NO MORE+

YOU TOSSED ME TO THE BOTTOM OF THE PIT,
INTO THE MURKY DARKNESS,
YOUR ANGER PULLED ME DOWN
LIKE ROARING WAVES+

YOU TOOK MY FRIENDS AWAY,
DISGRACED ME BEFORE THEM+
TRAPPED HERE WITH NO ESCAPE
I CANNOT SEE BEYOND MY PAIN+

LORD,
I CRY
OUT
TO YOU

LORD, I CRY OUT TO YOU ALL DAY,
MY HANDS KEEP REACHING OUT+
DO YOU WORK MARVELS FOR THE DEAD?
CAN SHADOWS RISE AND SING PRAISE?

IS YOUR MERCY SUNG IN THE GRAVE,
YOUR LASTING LOVE IN SHEOL?
ARE YOUR WONDERS KNOWN IN THE PIT?
YOUR JUSTICE, IN FORGOTTEN PLACES?

BUT I CRY OUT TO YOU, GOD,
EACH MORNING, PLEAD WITH YOU+
WHY DO YOU REJECT ME, LORD?
WHY DO YOU HIDE YOUR FACE?

I CRY
OUT
TO YOU,
GOD

WEAK SINCE CHILDHOOD,
I AM OFTEN CLOSE TO DEATH+
YOUR TORMENTS TRACK ME DOWN,
YOUR RAGE CONSUMES ME,
YOUR TRIALS DESTROY ME+

ALL DAY, THEY FLOOD AROUND ME,
PRESSING DOWN, CLOSING ME IN+
YOU TOOK MY FRIENDS FROM ME,
DARKNESS IS ALL I HAVE LEFT+

INTRODUCTION

Both love and tragedy abound in the world. The individuals with whom we inhabit this earth, and the societies in which we are gathered, surround us with grace, love, kindness and beauty. Yet we also encounter tragedy, disaster, violence and oppression. Newspapers and television broadcasts daily tell stories of violence against individuals, against races and groups, and against creation. We hear of political, economic and sexual oppression, of ecological destruction and of human and environmental tragedies. We recall momentous occasions of violence in the past — the Holocaust or the bombing of Hiroshima and Nagasaki, for example — and resolve that they are never to happen again.

We Christians know, even in times of violence and oppression, that God does not turn away from us. Nor does God turn away from any person who suffers or from any other part of creation that experiences disaster. So when we lament violence or disaster, we do not "grieve as those without hope" (1 Thessalonians 4:13): The life, suffering, death and resurrection of Jesus reveals to us God's steadfast love. The Spirit of God abides with us.

Prompted by that Spirit, we respond to tragedy, disaster, violence and oppression in prayer and in ritual, both alone and with others. We voice our prayer whether violence directly affects us, those we know, others in our city or nation, people elsewhere in the world, or when disaster strikes at creation itself. In our prayer we name and lament the violence and tragedy of our world; we confess it and condemn it. We stand in solidarity with and give voice to all who suffer. We express feelings of helplessness, sadness and anger. We remember and lament past occasions of violence and oppression and vow that they never again occur.

Empowered by our rites, as people of faith, we offer not only our prayers but also ourselves in the service of God and neighbor. When violence occurs or when disaster strikes, we do not sit idly by but engage in the work of healing, peace, justice, reconciliation and restoration. Such work grows out of and flows back into times of communal prayer and ritual.

In times past, Christians observed quarterly times of reflection, prayer and fasting called *ember days*. Until the reform of the Roman calendar in 1969, the Roman church designated as ember days the Wednesday, Friday and Saturday after the first Sunday of Lent, Pentecost, September 14 (Holy Cross) and December 13 (St. Lucy). When they were removed from the calendar, local conferences of bishops were encouraged to set aside regular days of prayer, fasting and almsgiving for various needs, in accord with local culture.

Ember days were not times of spiritual withdrawal from the concerns of the world but occasions for engagement and action as a result of prayer and fasting. Speaking more than 1500 years ago, Pope Leo I challenged the people of Rome:

> Let us adorn our fasting with works of mercy. Spend in good deeds what you withdraw from superfluity. Our fast must be turned into a banquet for the poor. Let us devote time and effort to the underprivileged, the widow and the orphan; let us show sympathy to the afflicted and reconcile the estranged; provide lodging for the wanderer and relieve the oppressed; give clothing to the naked and cherish the sick.[1]

In both prayer and action we live out our Christian vocation to care for our sisters and brothers who suffer and to care about tragedies that befall the whole of God's creation. This is our calling, this is our responsibility.

The first occasion for prayer in response to tragedy and oppression is our regular Sunday worship. Thus in the course of the year, the scriptures read in our liturgies tell of violence in the past: war and conquest, the slaughter of innocent children, rape and pillage, death and disease, poverty and slavery, famine and forced migration. In our worship, we place these in the context of the brutal death of Jesus Christ and his life-giving resurrection. And in preaching and prayer, we tell contemporary stories of similar tragedy and oppression and seek to respond to them in light of the scriptures.

Then, in the general intercessions (also known as the prayers of the faithful, the people, or the church), we name in prayer the needs of the world and of individuals. We do so with passion and in ways that call forth further response in action. When we beg, "Lord, hear our prayer!" or "Lord, have mercy!" we stand ready to be part of God's answer to our prayers by offering ourselves up as living sacrifices.

On other days, we may hold special services to name and lament specific instances of violence against humankind or against creation. Such days may be chosen in response to an unfolding tragedy in the community—a Friday set aside after the community learns of a series of rapes in its environs or a Wednesday evening after it learns of an oil spill, for example. Or, the days may be anniversaries of tragedies or disasters that have profoundly affected the community or the world: the anniversary of a civic disturbance caused by racism and poverty or the commemoration of the Holocaust, for example.

Some people today call for a restoration of quarterly occasions of prayer, fasting and action—ember days—so that this dimension of Christian life can more effectively enter into the rhythm of our individual and communal lives. The Roman Catholic bishops of the United States, in *Catholic Household Blessings and Prayers*, suggest that parishes and households set aside the following days for "fasting, works of charity and prayer" (page 186): August 6 and 9 (the anniversaries of the atomic bombings of Hiroshima and Nagasaki), the weekdays before Thanksgiving (the last Thursday of November), December 28 (the feast of the Holy Innocents) and Yom Hashoah (twelve days after Passover, a day of remembrance for the six million Jews who perished in the Holocaust).

Perhaps if dioceses, parishes and households discerned what anniversaries should be observed in a particular place and then scheduled them ahead of time, prepared the liturgies carefully and encouraged participation, a strong local tradition eventually would emerge. That tradition would then enable the community to respond to new tragedies that befell it or the world.

The liturgical books of the churches contain special prayers for many human needs and for the care of creation, though these are not widely known. Lists of such prayers in several contemporary worship books are given in chapter 11. The liturgical books also include services of penitence and of healing that might be appropriate for some instances of violence.

The range of both human needs and the needs of creation is great, and the groups and communities that may wish to gather in prayer around these needs are diverse. To try to present full and complete liturgies for specific needs and specific communities is, therefore, futile. Instead, this book offers local and community groups some resources that will help and encourage them to prepare rites and prayer in times of violence and disaster.

The resources provided include some general principles of preparing liturgy, as well as several kinds of orders of service that might be used. There are suggestions regarding scripture readings and psalms that might be appropriate, and model prayers of various kinds are also included.

Four specific liturgies are outlined and discussed in this book. They provide examples and starting places for those who prepare the rituals, and they may be suited to annual scheduling as part of the parish's liturgical life. These include a Holocaust remembrance liturgy, a liturgy responding to the abuse of nuclear energy, a service of lament for violence against creation and a service of lament for violence either against individuals or against groups. This latter service is appropriate in response to domestic or sexual violence; violence against refugees, exiles or homeless people; racial and ethnic discrimination; violence against aboriginal peoples, war or other forms of political and economic oppression.

This book is about liturgy — the communal worship of God — rather than about consciousness-raising or political rallies (valuable though these may be in other contexts). It is important, therefore, that those preparing liturgies for lamenting violence and tragedy study the general principles articulated in the first chapter. In liturgy, we enter into communion with each other and with our God, and in doing so we are transformed. That communion can be hindered if people arrive expecting to worship and instead are bombarded with information or are overtly urged to act in ways that may appear to be partisan. But that communion can be created and sustained when people arrive expecting to worship, and through carefully chosen music, words, gestures and postures, are led as one into the presence of the One who is steadfast mercy and love. Such a communion changes us. It empowers us and sends us forth from the liturgical assembly to be agents of reconciliation, healing and peace.

[1] An ember sermon of Pope Leo I, quoted in Pius Parsch, *The Church's Year of Grace,* vol. 1 (Collegeville: Liturgical Press 1959), 104.

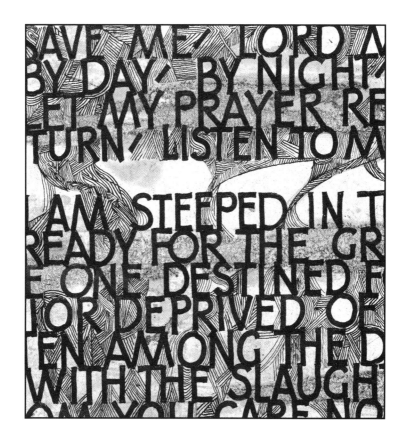

PREPARING THE LITURGY

I. GENERAL PRINCIPLES

The following general principles are important in preparing liturgies of lament.

- The liturgy will be prepared for *these* people on *this* occasion. A knowledge of *who* is gathering and *why* is essential.

- Gracious hospitality will be extended to all, and the full participation of persons with disabilities will be fostered.

- The liturgy will be worship of God. Education and consciousness-raising will result from worshiping God, but they are by-products, not primary goals.

- The liturgy will enable and encourage the full, conscious and active participation of all present.

- The liturgy will be enacted by whole persons — bodies, minds and souls — not just intellects. It therefore will not be didactic or overwhelmingly verbal.

- The language of liturgy is more often poetic than didactic. Inclusive language will be used.

- The liturgy will be musical. The singing of the whole assembly (hymns, acclamations and refrains) is primary.

- The place in which the liturgy takes place — the location, its arrangement and its decoration — will not hinder the participation of those present.

- The liturgy will carefully balance past, present and future dimensions of human experience. We always look to the past in the scripture readings and in other stories, but the liturgy is not simply history; we do not stay in the past. Such stories are always told to remind us of God's presence and action here in the present and tomorrow in the future. The future also needs to be named, the better to enable transformation. Rooted in the past, the liturgy happens in the present and is focused on the future.

2. QUESTIONS AND CONSIDERATIONS

These are some basic questions that those who prepare the liturgy need to ask and answer.

WHO?

Who will celebrate the liturgy — members of a particular group or members of an individual parish or congregation? Or is the liturgy intended to be ecumenical (interchurch), for members of neighboring Protestant, Orthodox and Roman Catholic parishes? Will it be an interfaith service in which Jews, Muslims, Buddhists, Hindus and others will be invited?

Under the appropriate circumstances, interchurch and interfaith liturgies are to be encouraged. However, they are a bit more complicated to plan than liturgies for a single congregation or a small group. Some principles and practical suggestions regarding interchurch and interfaith liturgies are provided in the appendix. Other faith communities also each have specific rules for ecumenical or interfaith gatherings, and these need to be investigated and respected.

Who will do the preparation? This question is especially relevant to interchurch and interfaith liturgies. If the idea for the liturgy comes from an ecumenical or interfaith group, then it is logical and appropriate for members of that group, representing the entire spectrum of churches or faiths involved, to prepare. In contrast, the idea may come from one parish, or one parish group, that wants to invite members of other churches and/or faiths. In this case, the host group will do the planning but will need to be especially sensitive to the intended guests.

WHY?

What is the need that will be brought to prayer and ritualized in this liturgy? What occasion or what instances of violence, disaster or oppression will be its focus? Name it, or them, clearly. Is this need experienced in broad terms — for example, environmental pollution in general — or is the focus more specific — such as the pollution of a particular lake or river? Has the violence been experienced immediately and individually by some of those present, or is it the experience of sisters and brothers outside the local community?

What is the sense of the community about this issue? How does the community feel about the issue? Is the community's sense or understanding of the issue different from that of those who will prepare this liturgy? Is there any chance of condescension on the part of those preparing? Does the community need to be informed of some facts before entering into the liturgy? How will this be done?

WHEN?

On what date will the liturgy be celebrated, and at what time of day? How long will it last? Do any other commitments of the participants require that it begin and end promptly as scheduled, or is it possible to be flexible with regard to time?

Is the liturgy a regularly scheduled occasion for lament for violence? Has your community decided to restore the ancient practice of ember days at the beginning of each season of the year (or at other appropriate times)? Or is the liturgy a response to the "signs of the times," a response to special needs that have arisen this month or this week and to which your community wishes to respond?

Is the date and time significant (an actual anniversary date, a symbolic day of the week, like Friday, or a symbolic hour, like sunrise or sunset)? Is it convenient for people to attend? Which of these is more important in this case? The crucifixion of Jesus on a Friday makes this day especially appropriate for fasting accompanied by a liturgy lamenting violence. The darkness of evening may be a reflection of the moral darkness of oppression and tragedy.

WHERE?

Where will the liturgy be celebrated — in the main place for worship, in a chapel or smaller room within the church, or in a school or home? Is the place accessible to those with mobility impairments? Is the space — and the seating available — large enough for the number of people expected? Is it too large? Can people be arranged so as to allow for a maximum sense of community, so that they are not made to feel like isolated individuals? Can participants see each other's faces as well as the faces of those in ministerial roles?

3. THE SHAPE OF THE LITURGY

Before choosing particular scripture readings, songs or gestures, the overall order of service — the outline or shape — of the liturgy needs to be decided. Rather than construct something arbitrary — "we'll do a reading, sing a song and then say some prayers" — look to the various ritual structures of the community's tradition first. These patterns of prayer and ritual will enable people to participate more fully, because they are familiar enough that people won't be wondering, "What comes next? Will I be uncomfortable with what comes next?"

Another reason to consult the traditional patterns is that many Christian churches share a common repertory of rites that may vary in detail but share essentially the same structure. Choosing and carefully adapting such rites will help people who may not normally worship together do so with ease and grace.

Here are some of the patterns of ritual prayer that are common within and among the Christian churches.

LITURGY OF THE WORD

We are familiar with this pattern from our Sunday liturgy: scripture readings, responses of various kinds, and preaching.

The basic dynamic is dialogue — proclamation and response. Proclamation comes through the liturgical reading of scripture, and response comes through silence, psalms, the profession of faith and the general intercessions. Preaching continues the proclamation, but it is also response.

In preparing a liturgy of the word, here are some questions to ask and answer: How many biblical passages are appropriate? Which ones? In what order should they be read? (Traditionally, passages are read in this order: first testament reading(s) [or one reading from the Acts of the Apostles or the Book of Revelation], second testament reading from one of the letters, one gospel reading; however, this may be adapted for a good reason.) Will each passage be read by a single reader or by two or more readers? Will the scriptures be dramatized, sung, spoken in sign language or proclaimed in other ways?

Response, both individual and corporate, may be expressed in several ways as well. Generally, there will be some silence after each reading. This is very important and should not be overlooked. Then there may be part or all of a psalm or biblical canticle, a song, a dance, poetry or contemporary readings; there may also be prepared or spontaneous prayers of confession, thanks, praise, or intercession; art or audiovisuals may also be used.

Preaching usually reflects on the readings, applies them to the current situation and tells appropriate contemporary stories. For liturgies of lament, this may be done by a single preacher, by shared preaching, by informal and spontaneous reflection by all participants, through the use of non-scriptural readings or poetry, by sharing in pairs or in other ways.

The readings, responses and preaching of a typical liturgy of the word often lead to the simple action of prayers of intercession in the form of a litany. Depending on the occasion and the assembly, other ritual actions may also follow the preaching: sharing a sign of peace, washing feet, anointing with oil, lighting or extinguishing candles, or sharing bread and wine or other food, for example. These actions need to be simple, authentic, and genuinely prayerful.

The liturgy of the word begins with some kind of introductory rite and concludes with some kind of concluding rite. See chapters 10 and 11 for more on these parts of the ritual.

PENITENTIAL SERVICES

Another liturgy for use in times of violence or disaster is found in the Roman Catholic liturgical book, *Rite of Penance,* appendix II. While this book is primarily about the three forms of the Roman Catholic sacrament popularly called "confession," appendix II provides a general pattern plus several sample "penitential celebrations" that do not involve sacramental confession and absolution. This kind of liturgy consists of an introductory rite, a liturgy of the word, a ritual action in response to God's word, and a concluding rite.

The action in response to God's word is two-fold: an examination of conscience and an act of repentance. Sprinkling the assembly with water, singing a litany for mercy, lighting a candle, placing on the altar a written resolution to perform an act of charity or justice, or collecting food for the poor are some of the acts of repentance that are suggested.

This order of service may be useful when the violence or disaster being named and lamented calls for penance. But penance here must be properly understood. Using a penitential service implies that the participants in the liturgy, either individually or as representatives of humankind, take responsibility for the violence or the disaster either because they cooperated with the evil (perhaps inadvertently) or because they failed to act to stop it.

An example of such a disaster might be environmental pollution. One parish is not solely responsible for the poisoning of the land, water and sky. In fact, no single member of the parish may be involved in any way in the dumping of hazardous wastes, the destruction of the rain forests or the killing of a river. But perhaps through a series of events, the members of the parish youth group learn and become concerned about the environmental crisis. Perhaps they begin to examine their own ways of living, their uses of consumable resources and their patterns of creating waste. They may begin a recycling effort in the neighborhood or participate in a local river clean-up project, but they want to do more. They want to bring their concerns to God, express sorrow for the desecration of the earth and vow (and be empowered) to make a change. A penitential service might be suitable in this situation.

A penitential liturgy must never be used to assign blame to people or to shame them. For example, this kind of rite would be inappropriate in a U.S. parish on August 6, the anniversary of the bombing of Hiroshima, if the intent of the planning group is to "teach" the rest of the parish that they should feel guilty. It would be appropriate, however, if the parish needed to come to a sense that this deed was done in its name and in some way to its benefit; and without passing arrogant judgment on those directly responsible, the parish now wishes to express sorrow for the consequences of that action and vow never again to let circumstances reach the point where the use of such destructive weapons is an option.

A penitential liturgy should never be used if there is any chance that it might imply that survivors of violence are to be blamed for their own oppression. Some other form of liturgy ought to be used instead.

LAMENT

A number of the psalms are known as psalms of lament, and these are subdivided into communal and individual psalms of lament; seven of these have traditionally been known as the penitential psalms. These are listed in Chapter 9 of the resource section.

In these psalms, the one who has experienced violence often expresses his or her innocence, names the oppressor, asks for punishment and appeals to God to intervene and deliver. We are never alone: Our suffering is God's suffering, too. These psalms also make us aware of all God's people around the world who are oppressed and hurting or who have been hurt and oppressed in the past. These psalms express a spectrum of feelings, including hurt, anger, denial and healing.

The psalms of lament are useful in preparing a liturgy in time of violence or disaster. The psalms themselves are appropriate texts to use, and the pattern they embody offers a guide for preparing a liturgy of lament. In general, this is the pattern of a psalm of lament:

Address to God
Complaint or lament
Confession of trust
Petition for help
Words of assurance
Vow of praise

An example of a liturgy patterned after a psalm of lament is given later in this book. Here, the "Address to God" serves as the introductory rite and the "Vow of praise" serves as a concluding blessing and dismissal.

It is most appropriate that the psalms of lament — and any other psalms as well — be sung, as this best respects their literary genre and their origin in the worship of Israel. They may be sung antiphonally, with the congregation divided into two choirs that take alternate verses; they may be sung responsorially, with the cantor or choir taking the verses and the entire assembly singing a response taken from the psalm text; or they may also be sung "straight-through" in unison. The music used may be psalm tones, through-composed tunes or metrical versions as found in various hymnals. Most or all of the psalms, with aids for singing them, may be found in *Lutheran Book of Worship* (1978), the Roman Catholic hymnal *Worship* (third edition, 1986), *The United Methodist Hymnal* (1989) and the Presbyterian *Book of Common Worship* (1993).

EVENING PRAYER

Two forms of evening prayer are outlined here. Most churches have orders of service for evening prayer in their liturgical books and/or hymnals, so consult those sources for more information. A good ecumenical resource is *Praise God in Song*, published by GIA (7404 South Mason Avenue, Chicago IL 60638).

A brief form of evening prayer would include these elements:

Light Service
    Acclamation, Hymn, Prayer of Thanksgiving
Incense Service
    Psalm 141, Prayer
Intercessions
    Litany of Intercession, Lord's Prayer
Concluding Rites
    Blessing, Sign of Peace

A longer, fuller evening prayer would contain these elements:

Light Service
    Opening verse, Evening hymn
Psalms
    Evening psalm (Psalm 141, for example), prayer
    Second psalm, prayer
    Third psalm or canticle of praise, prayer
Word of God
    Reading, Responsory

> Praise and Intercession
> > Canticle of Mary, Litany of Intercession, Lord's Prayer,
> > > Collect
> Concluding Rites
> > Blessing, Sign of Peace

Notice that both forms of evening prayer outlined above begin with a service of light: The Easter candle is either in place and lit when all gather, or it is carried (lit) into the darkened room after all have assembled. Then the light may be shared with all who are present, also holding candles. Acclamations and/or a hymn may be sung and a prayer giving thanks for the light in the darkness may be offered. These elements make up the introductory rite of evening prayer. Evening prayer concludes with a blessing and the sharing of the sign of peace.

For use as a liturgy of lament, one or the other structure may be adapted by choosing appropriate psalms, especially psalms of lament. Appropriate prayers may be chosen or composed, and intercessions may be composed that speak of the needs of society, individuals and creation.

PROCESSION

A liturgy of lament may be celebrated entirely or mostly while the assembly moves from place to place. This form of service may be especially appropriate for naming situations of oppression and violence in the local community. For example, the procession might go to places where violence has occurred, where discrimination against races and groups is practiced, or where economic or political oppression is exemplified. It might also go to places where good things are happening, in order to give thanks.

Such a liturgy is sometimes called a "way of the cross" or the "stations of the cross," especially when held during Lent or on Good

Friday and when it recalls the last hours of the life of Jesus. However, processional liturgies need not have this orientation.

If possible, the group sings appropriate songs or litanies while walking. Such music works best if it is memorized or can be easily learned; this way, it can be sung without much attention to books or papers. Roman Catholics traditionally sing the litany of the saints during processions; this is included as an appendix to the *Rite of Baptism for Children* and is in the sacramentary in the section on the Easter Vigil. Episcopal and Lutheran liturgical books contain another suitable litany, and music for this may be found in *Lutheran Book of Worship* and the *Episcopal Hymnal, 1982. The United Methodist Book of Worship* and the Presbyterian *Book of Common Worship* also contain appropriate litanies. Some of the music from the monastery of Taize, published by GIA (7404 South Mason Avenue, Chicago IL 60638), is also appropriate for use during processions.

The procession may begin and/or end in a church. It will need some kind of introductory rite when all are gathered and some kind of concluding rite when the final destination is reached. It may stop at predetermined, appropriate places for prepared and/or spontaneous prayers, short readings and reflections; these ought to be relatively brief. Banners might be carried, and the group might stop along the way to undertake some symbolic action. For example, a procession to places symbolizing the poisoning of the land, water and sky might include stops at places where trees are planted.

When preparing a procession, it is important to walk the route ahead of time. Make sure that it is accessible and that it can accommodate the number of people expected. If it is outdoors, you may need to obtain a parade permit or ask for traffic control help.

WHICH SHAPE?

How do those who are to prepare a liturgy of lament choose from among these basic shapes? Much depends on the needs and abilities of the local community that will celebrate the liturgy. There would seem to be no deep theological reasons for choosing one kind of liturgy over another, with the exceptions already noted concerning a penitential service. Instead, more pragmatic factors will influence this decision.

The first factor is familiarity. If something familiar will be most helpful, then the liturgy of the word model is the place to start. If there is a need or desire to do something new, then a liturgy based on the psalms of lament or a processional liturgy might be appropriate. Evening prayer will most likely be used by those communities that are already familiar with this form of liturgy.

Other factors that may influence the choice of what type of liturgy to choose include the following: the availability of good music resources, the abilities of the musicians, the familiarity of the worshipers with different kinds of music (especially psalmody), the time available for planning and preparation, and the experience of the group preparing the liturgy and the ease with which they write, adapt or borrow prayers from various sources.

4. BUILDING BLOCKS

Once the overall shape of the liturgy has been decided, specific decisions need to be made regarding its verbal, nonverbal and musical elements.

Greatest attention will be given to the core of the liturgy — the proclamation of scripture, the singing of psalms or the walking of the procession, for example. But liturgies also need beginnings and conclusions. The latter will be briefly addressed first.

BEGINNINGS AND ENDINGS

A liturgy's beginning — its *introductory rite* — is important. It gathers diverse individuals into an assembly and prepares that assembly to hear God's word by setting a certain tone for worship. A liturgy's ending — its *concluding rite* — is also important. It invokes God's blessing to empower the assembly to go forth "in peace to love and serve the Lord" by loving and serving others. No matter what type of liturgy is planned in response to violence or disaster, those doing the preparation would do well to carefully think through the beginning and ending of that liturgy.

Some liturgies, like evening prayer, have a particular kind of introductory rite — the service of candle lighting, for example. Most liturgies of the word begin with a song, a scriptural greeting or a call to worship, and then a short prayer offered by the leader. There may also be brief introductory remarks if these are necessary and appropriate. How many of these elements, and the order in which they will be used, is for local planners to decide. Roman Catholics, for example, are more familiar with the scriptural greeting; Protestants traditionally use a call to worship.

Liturgies often conclude with a benediction or blessing, a dismissal, a commissioning or sending forth, and a song.

NONVERBAL ELEMENTS

Worship takes place in space and time and engages the whole person (not just the intellect). It is a human activity that utilizes material things, things that God created. In worship, God communicates with us and we communicate with God and with each other nonverbally as well as verbally. Because the nonverbal dimension of worship is sometimes neglected in favor of the verbal elements, it is considered here first.

Space. Besides being the proper size for the gathering and accessible to those with mobility impairments, the space in which the liturgy will take place ought to be arranged to facilitate the full, conscious and active participation of all present.

Is the space hospitable? That is, is it a welcoming environment? Is there room for informal gathering before and after the liturgy? Are there lavatories (stocked with facial tissues, drinking water and cups) nearby?

Does the space foster community among those present? Is seating arranged so that people are aware of each other and so that a sense of unity is manifested? Can members of the assembly be seated so as to see each other's faces rather than the backs of each other's heads? Are leaders and other ministers able to function, yet still be part of the community as a whole?

Is the space suitable for the liturgical action of the assembly? Is it good for singing? Can everyone see and hear? Can they change posture and move about?

Embodiment. Worship involves the whole person — not only the mind and heart but the body as well. Good liturgy is scriptural, musical and physical, involving the five senses through judicious use of material objects (such as candles, water, incense or oil), postures (such as standing, kneeling, prostrating), gestures (such as bowing, raising up hands in supplication, or exchanging a sign of peace) and movements (such as moving in procession). Given the nature of the assembly and the shape of the liturgy, which of these postures and gestures might be appropriate?

The material objects used in liturgy should speak for themselves: If a symbol needs to be explained while it is being used, it is probably not worth using in that context. A material object will speak powerfully if it is in proper scale: A dinner table candle carried into the midst of 50 people will not embody light shattering the darkness as much as a three-foot Easter candle will. Use things — water, oil, incense — abundantly. But before planning to borrow symbols from other faiths or cultures, see the section on authenticity, in this chapter.

VERBAL ELEMENTS

Liturgies of lament may include long or short scripture readings, psalms or portions of psalms. The readings may be proclaimed by one or more readers, depending on the length and genre of the passages. Psalms may be sung responsorially, antiphonally or in a metrical version, or they may be spoken in various ways. For more on psalm singing, see the section on music that follows. To help find appropriate scriptures, see chapter 9. Look in your lectionary, too. The amount of scripture that you use will depend on the nature of the assembly, the shape of the liturgy and the circumstances under which the liturgy is celebrated.

Short prayers of petition, intercession, confession, thanksgiving and praise may be borrowed from liturgical books and other resources or may be composed for the occasion. Longer prayers may include litanies and responsorial prayers. Finally, liturgical dialogues probably will be included.

When preparing texts for a liturgy, remember that the language of liturgy is more narrative and poetic than the rational and didactic language of textbooks. Narrative and poetry are used because they are best able to express the inexpressible, to express feeling in addition to communicating concepts and ideas.

Avoid drowning the ritual in talk. All the words used — especially announcements, directions or remarks — need to be thought out carefully.

Care also needs to be taken that the language used is inclusive. This is a matter of justice and reconciliation. For scripture, the *New Revised Standard Version* is particularly useful and is approved for liturgical use by the Roman Catholic bishops of the United States and Canada.

MUSIC IN LITURGY

By nature, liturgy is musical. Singing by the whole assembly (hymns, acclamations and refrains) is primary. Depending on the culture of the assembly, pieces performed by a choir or a soloist may be important ways for the assembly to participate through listening, clapping or swaying. Or, they may be secondary or even of little importance.

Music functions in various ways in a single liturgy. Sometimes singing is done for the sake of singing (an opening or gathering song, for example). Here, a song is best done in its entirety. At other times, singing (or instrumental music) accompanies a ritual action (walking in procession, for example). Here, the music lasts as long as the action that it accompanies. When singing accompanies a ritual action, something that can be sung without using a book or sheet of paper is ideal.

Finally, singing without the accompaniment of musical instruments is often striking and appropriate for penitential services.

Because there are so many hymnals in use, plus a great wealth of songs not in regular hymnals, few specific suggestions can be made in this book; rely on local church musicians and the resources that the assembly knows and uses in regular worship.

SILENCE

Communal silence is an important yet often overlooked part of liturgy. It is not the unavoidable "dead time" that occurs in the theatre between scene changes. Nor is it even the hushed anticipation of a concert audience awaiting the next movement. Instead, it is deliberate quiet, held in common, so that the assembly can ponder together what it has just proclaimed and heard. Some opportunities for silence in liturgies of lament occur after a scripture reading; after a homily, sermon, testimony or reflection; after a psalm; or after the invitation "Let us pray." Different ministers are responsible for presiding over silence. They are usually the presider (after saying "Let us pray"; after the psalm and before the psalm prayer; after the homily and before the next action) or the song leader (after the reading and before she or he begins the psalm).

When members of the assembly are invited to offer spontaneous prayers, reflections or responses, they may at first respond in silence and only after several moments respond in speech. They may not be moved to pray aloud at all. In that case, the presider must resist the temptation to fill the silence with his or her own speech. If no one chooses to offer prayers, reflections or responses aloud, after a respectable period of silence the liturgy continues. It is important that the ministers be comfortable with this possibility so that the silence does not engender confusion.

AUTHENTICITY

In order to enable an assembly to worship "in spirit and in truth," planners need to be concerned with the authenticity of the words, music, actions and signs that are used in the liturgy. Are the verbal and nonverbal elements of the liturgy authentic in the sense that they spring up from the assembly's deepest experiences of suffering, sorrow and God's presence? Is there consistency between the liturgy and the rest of life, or is there a chance for hypocrisy? Are gimmicks being avoided?

When thinking of borrowing sacred texts, music, actions or objects (such as blowing a shofar or using eagle feathers to spread incense smoke) from other cultures, churches or faiths, these questions need to answered: Is the original meaning of the text, music, action or object understood? Does the text, music, action or object make sense in this particular context? Will the assembly be able to enter into the experience, or will it be distracted by novelty? Will any of the participants experience its use as a sacrilege? Will people who hear about the liturgy later be scandalized by the use of the text, music, action or object?

LEADERSHIP, MINISTRY AND PARTICIPATION

Liturgy is the work of the whole church — head and members, Christ and ourselves. This means that the assembly is the primary minister of a liturgy. All the members of the assembly should be encouraged to participate as fully as possible; the planners will want to be conscious of the different ways this can be accomplished.

Participation includes our external actions during worship: what we say, sing and do. But it also includes our internal appropriation of the meaning of these actions: We mean what we say, sing and do. Participation engenders among worshipers a communion that we seal by living out the meaning of our corporate worship. Thus we enter into communion with God.

This communion does not mean that everyone does everything in unison. Many persons, according to their gifts and talents, will carry out individual ministries for the benefit of the whole.

A general rule is that no one person will exercise more than one specific ministry: The song leader doesn't also do the scripture readings, and the person presiding doesn't lead the singing.

The various ministries need to be done well; those chosen to fill them need to have the requisite skills and training. In particular, does the presider know how to invite and encourage the sharing of reflections and prayers that are suggested here in the various model liturgies? Is he or she familiar with the different dynamics of small and large groups in this regard? Is the presider comfortable with silence? Does he or she know what to do if no one shares?

Does the song leader, besides having the requisite technical skills, know how to lead without dominating the assembly's singing? Do the readers understand the scriptures they are proclaiming? Are the ushers prepared to welcome visitors and assist people who may need help?

Although the first responsibility of those preparing the liturgy should be to find people capable of these services, ministerial roles also should be distributed — to the extent possible — so that they reflect a balance among old and young, men and women and the various races and ethnic heritages of the whole assembly.

FINAL DETAILS

There are always a number of details that need to be considered when preparing a liturgy, especially a liturgy of lament.

What adjustments need to be made if the size of the assembly is bigger or smaller than anticipated? For example, some music is more or less accessible for small groups, and the sharing of reflections and spontaneous prayers of intercession might be easier in small groups than in a large assembly. What alternatives will be available at the last minute?

Who will obtain, or who will provide, any material objects needed in the liturgy?

How will publicity be handled?

Will orders of service or similar participation aids be needed by, and provided for, the entire assembly? What will these contain? (Liturgy is not a choral reading session; in general, provide only the texts needed.) Who will prepare them?

What music is needed? Are hymnals available? If copies are made, what copyright permissions are required? Who will obtain these?

If informational materials are to be made available, can they be placed somewhere accessible, such as the gathering space, and not clutter up the place for the liturgy?

If any special implements or decorations are to be used, will they help the assembly enact the liturgy, or are they gimmicks? Are they beautiful and evocative, or prosaic and didactic?

If audiovisual materials are going to be used, what equipment and resources will be needed? Are there spare bulbs, fuses and extension cords available? Who will set these up — prior to the liturgy — and see that everything works?

What rehearsals are needed for musicians, leaders and other ministers? Practice and rehearsal are needed not to reach perfection or to be fussy but to allow everyone present to enter into prayer with minimum distraction.

What costs will be incurred, and how will they be covered?

L I T U R G I E S   F O R   S P E C I F I C

O C C A S I O N S

To illustrate the process of planning liturgies of lament, four services for specific occasions are given here in outline. Also, some rationale for each liturgy is given, and references are made to scripture readings, psalms and prayers either listed or given in full in the resource section, chapters 9 – 12.

These outlines need to be adapted to the particular assembly that will be celebrating the liturgy.

5. IN MEMORY OF THE HOLOCAUST:

LEST WE FORGET

INTRODUCTORY RITE

> Greeting *and/or*
> Call to Worship
> Welcome and Introduction
> Song
> Opening Prayer

WORD AND RESPONSE

> Scripture and silence
> Response
> > Psalm 77 (or 88) *or*
> > Survivors' accounts *or*
> > Song

> Scripture and silence
> Response
> > Responsive prayer *or*
> > Reflections on the Holocaust *or*
> > Song

> Sermon

SUMMONS TO REMEMBER

> Lighting of memorial candles
> Standing in solidarity
> Invitation
> Mourner's Kaddish *and*
>   El Male Rachamin *or*
> Psalm 121

CONCLUDING RITE

> Blessing
> Commissioning
> Song

NOTES

This liturgy could be used on Yom Hashoah, when the Jews commemorate the Holocaust twelve days after Passover, or on some other appropriate occasion. It may be celebrated in several ways: by Christians alone, by Christians with a few Jewish guests or by a joint Christian–Jewish group.

In this service, participants are called to remember the great tragedy of the Holocaust, both for its own sake and so that some similar massacre will not be permitted to occur in the future. Memory is kept of the Jews who were killed, but the Holocaust is a great Christian tragedy as well; for it was in traditionally Christian nations that the killing took place. Many Christians also died in the death camps, and they too are remembered. Participants are called to face the darkness — within themselves, within the churches, and within the Christian tradition — that makes the Holocaust a dark night of faith for Jews and Christians alike.

The Shape of the Liturgy The first part of this liturgy is a liturgy of the word, with two scripture readings, responses after each reading, and preaching. Suggested readings are listed in the resource section; suggested psalms are given in the outline. The introductory rite is quite simple — the ministers are in place before the liturgy begins, and at the appointed time a greeting is given.

The second part contains the symbolic action of lighting candles in remembrance of the dead and gives some appropriate prayers. The concluding rite is a blessing and commissioning.

Texts Texts that might be appropriate for the opening and closing sections of this liturgy, for the opening prayer and for the responsive prayer after the second scripture reading may be found in the resource section. Also, appropriate songs may be sung as responses to the readings; these can be songs about the Holocaust, if these are known.

As one response to the first scripture reading, stories of the Holocaust may be told by survivors or by others who carry on the memories of the survivors. Alternatively, excerpts from published accounts of the Holocaust may be read.

As one response to the second scripture reading, published reflections on the Holocaust may be read. Alternatively, such passages may be incorporated into the preaching.

Several resources for stories and reflections are in chapter 12.

Ritual Actions The symbolic action that follows the scripture readings is the lighting of candles in memory of those killed. This might be done by a minister or by representatives from the assembly, lighting six candles in memory of the six million Jews — children, women and men — who were systematically murdered. It might also include lighting five additional candles in memory of the five million non-Jews — Christians and others — who were murdered.

This act of remembrance is a profound form of resistance to oppression and a radical act of solidarity. Participants resist the forces of forgetfulness and denial. They also act in solidarity with the living and the dead and affirm the light of faith in each other.

Following the lighting of candles, a Jewish leader, if present, may lead all in the Mourner's Kaddish, and a Jewish cantor, if present, may sing the El Male Rachmin, a song for the dead; these texts are given in the resource section. If these are not used, Psalm 121 may be sung or said responsively.

At the end, in addition to an appropriate blessing and commissioning, the prayer of St. Francis may be sung or spoken in unison as a form of commitment.

6. IN MEMORY OF THE BOMBING OF HIROSHIMA AND NAGASAKI: LEST WE FORGET

INTRODUCTORY RITE

> Greeting *and/or*
> Call to Worship
> Song
> Opening Prayer

TELLING THE STORY

> Account of Hiroshima and Nagasaki
> Silence
> Responses

CONFESSION

> Psalm 51 (or 38 or 130)
> Call to Conversion
> Scripture and silence
> Intercessions
> Song

CALL TO BE PEACEMAKERS

> Scripture and silence
> Reflection/preaching
> Naming signs of hope
> Prayer

CONCLUDING RITE

> Blessing
> Dismissal
> Song

NOTES

This liturgy could be used on August 6 or 9, the anniversaries of the atomic bombings of Hiroshima and Nagasaki, respectively, or when radioactive materials become a threat to human health or to creation.

In their 1983 pastoral letter *The Challenge of Peace*, the Roman Catholic bishops of the United States wrote:

> After the passage of nearly four decades and a concomitant growth in our understanding of the ever growing horror of nuclear war, we must shape the climate of opinion which will make it possible for our country to express profound sorrow over the atomic bombing in 1945. Without that sorrow, there is no possibility of finding a way to repudiate future use of nuclear weapons.

THE SHAPE OF THE LITURGY

The shape of this liturgy is somewhat unusual in that the telling of the human story of atomic bombing precedes the proclamation of scripture rather than follows it. This dynamic seems especially appropriate when commemorating an event that happened long ago and far away; the focus of the liturgy needs to be sharpened and clarified before we get very far into it, so that the scripture readings become more forceful and moving with the human story already told, at least in part. The telling of the story is followed by confession, using one of the penitential psalms. Then comes the liturgy of the word and a simple concluding rite.

Texts The story of the bombing of Hiroshima and Nagasaki, and of the suffering of the inhabitants of those cities, may be told in a variety of ways. Pictures of the bombed cities and its inhabitants may be shown, published accounts may be read, or poems and other interpretations of these events may be shared. How this might be done will depend on the availability of materials, on the size of the group and on the arrangement of seating.

Participants may be invited to state their feelings about the bombings of the Japanese cities, about the use of nuclear weapons in the years since 1945 or about more recent disasters involving nuclear power, such as Chernobyl. They may also be invited to imagine what it might have been like to experience the bombings or Chernobyl. Periods of silent reflection may follow.

The second half of the liturgy (call to conversion; call to be peacemakers) takes the form of a liturgy of the word. Suggested scripture readings are given in the resource section. A sermon or homily may be preached, participants may share their reflections, or both. Suggested prayers, as well as texts for the opening and closing, may be found in the resource section.

Ritual Action After the homily, participants may name signs of hope with respect to the threat of nuclear bombs and weapons of mass destruction. This spontaneous naming is a prophetic sign that the seeds of peace have been planted and that we need only tend them. This also could be done as a litany, with a simple response (such as "We thank you, Lord!") sung or said after each sign of hope is named.

7. LAMENT FOR VIOLENCE AGAINST CREATION

INTRODUCTORY RITE

>   Greeting *and/or*
>   Call to Worship
>   Song
>   Prayer

THE GOOD NEWS OF GOD'S CREATION

>   Scripture
>   Response
>>   Psalm 103:1-23 *and/or*
>>   Contemporary reading and reflection
>>   *and/or*
>>   Hold up the goodness of creation *and/or*
>>   Prayer *and/or*
>>   Song

ABUSE OF GOD'S CREATION

Scripture

Response

> Lament: Jeremiah 14: 1-9 *and/or*
>
> Contemporary reading and reflection
> *and/or*
>
> Show how creation has been abused
> *and/or*
>
> Prayer *and/or*
>
> Song

TOWARD THE HEALING OF CREATION

Scripture

Response

> Psalm 104:24-35 *and/or*
>
> Contemporary reading and reflection
> *and/or*
>
> Plant a seed or a sapling *and/or*
>
> Prayer *and/or*
>
> Song

CONCLUDING RITE

> Blessing
> Dismissal
> Song

NOTES

This liturgy could be used to lament violence against creation in a very general way or to name and condemn specific instances of violence. "Creation" is used here instead of "environment" to include humankind as well as animals and all living things, the earth, the waters and the atmosphere.

The Shape of the Liturgy This is a liturgy of the word with three sections, each containing a scripture reading and several possible responses. The liturgy begins by naming the goodness of creation; then it speaks of human abuse of creation and finally looks to the future healing of creation.

Texts Suggestions for scriptures, prayer texts, greetings and calls to worship are in the resource section. Contemporary poetry or other writing may also be used in response to scripture (see following section); check the local library.

Ritual Action Five kinds of responses to the scriptures are suggested: a psalm, a reading from a contemporary source and/or shared reflections, a nonverbal action, a prayer, or a song. Planners will have to decide how many of these should be used for each reading. To help the rhythm of the liturgy, it would be best to do the same kind and number of responses for each of the three readings.

Because of the amount of scripture proposed here, silence between the reading and the response, and between each unit of reading/response(s), is essential. See page 26. A leisurely, reverent pace is important so that this liturgy isn't experienced as a torrent of words.

A psalm sung in response to a reading is familiar to most Christians. Suggested psalms are listed in the outline. Or, contemporary readings and poetry having to do with the focus of each section might be read. Instead, or in addition, one or more participants may share their reflections. The presider should see page 26.

Nonverbal response also might follow. In the section titled "The Good News of God's Creation," for example, one or more dimensions of creation may be reverently passed from person to person—flowers, fruits, vegetables or a pitcher of water, for example.

In the second section, concrete examples of how creation has been abused might be shown using photos or film, or by having polluted water in a bowl. For the third section, some symbolic action that provides an example of the healing of creation may be carried out — planting some seeds or a sapling, for example. In this case, everything must be carefully prepared ahead of time so that the action can be done without confusion. Directions need to be thought out and written down so that words of explanation do not drown the ritual.

Short prayers may also constitute appropriate responses, just as collect prayers are used after each reading and psalm at the Easter Vigil. Having been seated for the reading, the assembly could be invited — through gesture and without words — to stand for the collect. The prayer could be sung.

Finally, appropriate songs might also constitute responses in each section, especially if a psalm has not been sung.

8. LAMENT FOR VIOLENCE AGAINST INDIVIDUALS OR GROUPS

INTRODUCTORY RITE

> Greeting *and/or*
> Call to Worship
> Song

COMPLAINT

> Psalm
> > Individuals: 22 (or 6, 102, 55)
> > Groups: 79 (or 80)
> Stories of contemporary violence
> Silence
> Prayer

PETITION AND ASSURANCE

> Psalm
> > Individuals: 7 (or 36, 59, 69, 71)
> > Groups: 85 (or 94)

Stories of contemporary healing and hope
Anointing with oil
Prayer
Song

TRUST AND PRAISE

Psalm
Individuals: 86 (or 13, 31, 42 – 43, 56)
Groups: 126 (or 12, 129)
Dreams for an alternative future
Circle dance or hold hands
Prayer

CONCLUDING RITE

Blessing
Dismissal
Song

NOTES

This liturgy could be used to lament any kind of violence against individuals. It is appropriate, for example, in the event of domestic, sexual or physical violence of various kinds.

This liturgy could also be used to lament violence against groups of people, such as those who endure racial and ethnic discrimination, homophobia, hunger, poverty, political and economic oppression, or war. It is appropriate for lamenting the violence committed against refugees, exiles, aboriginal peoples or people who are homeless.

It is essential that those preparing this liturgy know the nature of the assembly that will celebrate it. The violence might have been experienced personally by some or all of those present, which is a somewhat different situation than when no participant has actually experienced it.

The Shape of the Liturgy The shape of the liturgy is that of lament: It follows the pattern of the psalms of lament. For more on this, see pages 16–18.

Texts The suggested scripture passages are not prose readings but psalms that might be sung (or said) responsorially, antiphonally or in unison. Specific examples of appropriate individual and communal psalms of lament are given in the outline above. Planners might want to select portions of each psalm or use entire psalms.

The prayers suggested in the resource section are based on the ministry of Jesus as recounted in the gospels. Because the psalms of the Hebrew scriptures form a large part of this liturgy, the shorter prayers that are included are inspired by the Christian scriptures.

Suggestions for the opening and closing parts of the liturgy may be found in the resource section or composed by local planners.

Ritual Action Following each of the three psalms, stories of contemporary violence against individuals may be told by participants. Thus, stories of violence in our world today may be recounted by people who have experienced violence as well as by others. Similarly, stories of healing following violence may be shared, and stories of hope with respect to the prevention of violence, the conversion of those who do violence, and appropriate changes in our society may be recounted. Finally, participants may share their dreams for a world in which violence is not committed against individuals or groups of people—and their dreams for how this might be achieved.

Telling stories of personal domestic or sexual violence may require a level of trust that needs to be gained as well as respected. Leaders and participants should be prepared for the shedding of tears and consider this a blessing.

After the sharing of contemporary stories of violence, a good response would be a healthy period of silence. After stories of healing and hope, those who have experienced violence may, if they consent, be anointed with oil or touched gently in a healing manner. This will require careful discernment: Some survivors of rape or torture find it traumatic to be touched by strangers. As members of a violent society, all may be anointed with oil or touched, if this seems appropriate.

A number of ministers appropriate to the size of the assembly need to be trained well ahead of time as to how the anointing or laying on of hands will actually take place. Olive oil or any natural vegetable oil would be appropriate; a natural balsam or essence oil may be added for scent. (Avoid chemical additives in case some people are allergic.)

Finally, to express solidarity and commitment to the establishment of healing communities, all might join hands and participate in a simple circle dance. Alternatively, all might form a circle (if this is possible in the space being used) and hold hands while singing a simple refrain, such as "We Shall Overcome."

Short prayers might also follow each set of stories. Appropriate songs might be used to conclude each section, as well as to begin and end.

AN ALTERNATIVE APPROACH

Another kind of liturgy of lament for violence against individuals or groups may be devised by modifying the outline in this chapter. In such a liturgy, the first psalm of lament is replaced with a prose scripture reading, such as one telling a story of sexual abuse (see page 53). In addition, the third psalm of lament is replaced by a modern composition, for example, some of the laments in Miriam Therese Winter's *Woman Prayer Woman Song* (Oak Park IL: MeyerStone 1987).

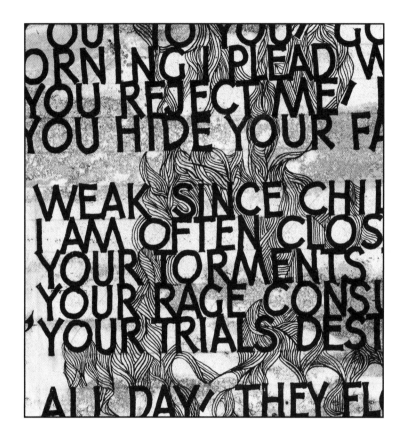

PART III

RESOURCES

Four kinds of resources are provided in the following chapters:

9. A listing of scripture readings and psalms of lament

10. Complete prayers and other liturgical texts

11. A listing of prayers in the liturgical books of several churches

12. A listing of other published resources (this list is only suggestive, and not at all complete)

9. SCRIPTURE READINGS

AND PSALMS

HOLOCAUST

Genesis 9:8 – 15   The covenant with Noah.

Deuteronomy 5:1 – 14   The first three commandments.

Joshua 4:19 – 24   Entrance into the promised land.

Micah 4:1 – 5   Vision of peace.

Leviticus 19:13 – 18   Justice toward one another.

Genesis 4:2b – 10   Cain and Abel.

Lamentations 3:46 – 66   Suffering and lamentation.

Isaiah 52:13 — 53:13   Fourth servant song.

Matthew 25:31 – 46   The last judgment.

James 1:19 – 25   True religion.

Mark 2:28 – 34   The greatest commandment.

1 John 4:16 – 21   Perfect love.

James 3:13 – 18   Real wisdom and its opposite.

HIROSHIMA AND NAGASAKI

Genesis 4:1 – 11   Cain and Abel.

Exodus 20:1 – 21   The decalogue.

Isaiah 24:1 – 23   Judgment on the earth for breaking the
   covenant.

Hosea 6:1 – 6   Repentance, love, not holocausts.

Matthew 2:1 – 18   The slaughter of the innocents.

Matthew 25:31 – 66   I was hungry.

Revelation 7:9 – 17   These are the ones who have come through
   the great tribulation.

Psalm 85   Prayer for peace.

Isaiah 61   The good news of change and transformation.

Ezekiel 34:25 – 30   Prophecy of peace.

Micah 6:1 – 8   Act justly.

Matthew 5:1 – 12   The beatitudes.

Luke 6:27 – 35   Love of enemies.

James 2:12 – 17   Faith and good works.

1 John 1:5 – 7   Live in the light.

CREATION

The goodness of creation:

Genesis 1:1 – 2:4   The first account of creation.

Genesis 9:1 – 17   The covenant with Noah.

Deuteronomy 11:8 – 21   The richness of the promised land.

Job 38 – 39   The wisdom of the creator.

Luke 12:22 – 31 or Matthew 6:25 – 34   The birds of the air and
   the grasses of the fields.

Colossians 1:15 – 17   Christ, the first-born of all creation.

The abuse of God's creation:

Genesis 3:17 – 19   Brambles and thistles.

Deuteronomy 29:22 – 28   Plagues on the land.

Jeremiah 2:1 – 13   Defiling the land.

Jeremiah 12:7 – 13   Devastation of the land.

Matthew 24:15 – 25   The tribulation of Jerusalem.
Revelation 8:6 – 13   The end of the world.

Toward the healing of creation:
Genesis 2:5 – 16   The garden of Eden.
Genesis 9:1 – 17   The covenant with Noah.
Exodus 23:10 – 12   The sabbatical year and the sabbath.
Leviticus 25:1 – 19   The sabbath and jubilee of the land.
Isaiah 41:17 – 20   Miracles of the new exodus.
Romans 8:18 – 27   Creation is waiting for the fullness of time.

SEXUAL ABUSE

Judges 19:1 – 30   The unnamed and dismembered woman.
2 Samuel 13:1 – 22   The rape of princess Tamar.
Genesis 19:1 – 10   Lot offers his daughter to rapists.
Judges 29:11 – 40   The sacrifice of Jephthah's daughter.

ABORIGINAL PEOPLES

1 Kings 21:1 – 16   Ahad steals Naboth's land.
Leviticus 25:23 – 29   Land ownership and year of jubilee.
Deuteronomy 14:28 – 29   Concern for the oppressed and poor.
Exodus 16:15a – 21   Manna from heaven.
Genesis 1:1 – 2:4   The beginning.
Jeremiah 31:31 – 34   God makes a new covenant.
Amos 5:21 – 24   Let justice flow.
Psalm 95:1 – 4   Defeat does not come to those who trust God.
Psalm 146:7 – 8   The Lord is constant in love.
1 Corinthians 12:3 – 13   The gifts of the Spirit.

PSALMS OF LAMENT AND PENITENCE

Scholars do not completely agree on the classification of these psalms. The following list is based on the composite listing of three authorities:

Bernhard W. Anderson. *Out of the Depths: The Psalms Speak for Us Today* (Philadelphia: Westminster Press 1983).

John F. Craghan. *The Psalms: Prayers for the Ups, Downs and In-Betweens of Life. A Literary-Experiential Approach* (Wilmington: Michael Glazier 1985).

Claus Westermann. *Praise and Lament in the Psalms* (Edinburgh: T. & T. Clark 1965, 1981).

Communal Laments

PSALM

12	On every side the wicked prowl.
44	Because of you we are being killed all day long.
58	Surely there is a God who judges on earth.
60	You have made your people suffer hard things.
74	O God, why do you cast us off forever?
79	The nations have come into your inheritance.
80	You have fed them with the bread of tears.
83	O God, do not keep silence.
85	That God's glory may dwell in our land.
89	(verses 35-51) Will you hide yourself forever?
90	Teach us to count our days.
94	How long shall the wicked exult?
123	We have had more than enough of contempt!
126	Those who sow in tears.
129	Often have they attacked me from my youth.
137	On the willows there we hung up our harps.

Individual Laments

PSALM

3   Many are rising against me.

4   I will both lie down and sleep in peace.

5   Their throats are open graves.

7   Save me from all my pursuers.

9   (and psalm 10) Why do you hide yourself in time of trouble?

13   Will you forget me for ever?

14   The fool. (Same as psalm 53)

17   Guard me as the apple of your eye.

22   My God, why have you forsaken me?

25   For you I wait all day long.

26   I have walked in my integrity.

27   (verses 7-14) Let your heart take courage.

28   Do not drag me away with the wicked.

31   Into your hand I commit my spirit.

35   Contend, O Lord, with those who contend with me.

36   Do not let the foot of the arrogant tread on me.

39   I held my peace to no avail.

40   (verses 12-17) Evils have encompassed me without number.

41   Heal me, for I have sinned against you.

42   (and psalm 43) Why are you cast down, O my soul?

52   Why do you boast, O mighty ones?

53   (A variant of psalm 14)

54   Save me, O God, by your name.

55   O that I had wings like a dove.

56   When I am afraid, I put my trust in you.

57   I will awake the dawn.

59   You, O God, are my fortress.

61   The rock that is higher than I.

63   My soul thirsts for you.

64   Hide me from the secret plots of the wicked.

69   I have come into deep waters.

70   Be pleased, O God, to deliver me.

71   Upon you I have leaned from my birth.

77   I am so troubled that I cannot speak.

86   In the day of my trouble I call on you.

88   Why do you hide your face from me?

89   (verses 38-51) Will you hide yourself forever?

109   They reward me evil for good.

120   Among those who hate peace.

139   Where can I go from your spirit?

140   Along the road they have set snares for me.

141   Let my prayer be counted as incense.

142   When my spirit is faint.

Penitential Psalms

PSALM

6   My soul is struck with terror.

32   You forgave the guilt of my sin.

38   There is no health in my bones because of my sin.

51   Create in me a clean heart, O God.

102   I mingle tears with my drink.

130   Out of the depths I cry to you.

143   Do not enter into judgment with your servant.

Elsewhere in Scripture

Other psalms of lament are found outside of the book of psalms, for example:

Jeremiah 11:18 – 12:6   A gentle lamb led to the slaughter.

Jeremiah 15:10 – 21   I sat alone.

Jeremiah 17:14 – 18   Do not become a terror to me.

Jeremiah 18:19 – 23   Is evil a recompense for good?

Jeremiah 20:7 – 13   Something like a burning fire.

Jeremiah 20:14 – 18   Why did I come forth from the womb?

Lamentations 3   I am one who has seen affliction.

IO. PRAYERS AND
OTHER LITURGICAL TEXTS

GREETINGS

The presider gives the greeting and the assembly responds, "And also with you."

1   May the God of all consolation
        be with you.

2   May the God of peace
        be with you.

3   May the God of all creation
        be with you.

4   May the God of compassion and justice
        be with us.

5   May the God of peace and mercy
        be with us.

6   May the Compassionate One,
        who feels our pain and cries with us in our passion,

and the Just One, who rages with us against
the injustice of our experience,
be with you.

(From Denise Davis Taylor, Edmonton)

CALLS TO WORSHIP

1   Presider:

In silence let us seek God's presence.

(pause)

or

In silence let us face the darkness
in ourselves and in our churches,
in our community and in our country.

(pause)

or

In this act of silent remembrance, let us resolve
that never again shall we remain silent
in the face of darkness.

(pause)

All:

Search me, O God, and know my heart!
Try me and know my thoughts!
See if there be any hurtful way in me,
   and lead me in the way everlasting.
For your name's sake. Amen.

2   Presider or All: The earth dries up and withers,
the world languishes and withers;
the heavens languish together with the earth.
The earth lies polluted under its inhabitants;

for they have transgressed laws,
violated the statutes,
broken the everlasting covenant.

3   Presider: In the beginning, God created the heavens and
             the earth.
All: AND GOD SAW THAT IT WAS GOOD.

Presider: God said, Let there be light.
All: AND GOD SAW THAT IT WAS GOOD.

Presider: Let the waters be gathered together,
             and let the dry land appear.
All: AND GOD SAW THAT IT WAS GOOD.

Presider: Let the earth put forth vegetation.
All: AND GOD SAW THAT IT WAS GOOD.

Presider: Let the waters bring forth swarms of living
             creatures.
All: AND GOD SAW THAT IT WAS GOOD.

Presider: Let the earth bring forth living creatures of
             every kind.
All: AND GOD SAW THAT IT WAS GOOD.

Presider: Let us make humankind in our image,
             according to our likeness.
All: AND GOD SAW THAT IT WAS GOOD.

Presider: And God rested on the seventh day.
All: AMEN!

4   Presider: Be gracious to me, O Lord,
                 for I am languishing;

All: O LORD, HEAL ME, FOR MY BONES ARE
      SHAKING WITH TERROR.

Presider: Turn, O Lord, save my life;

All: DELIVER ME FOR THE SAKE OF YOUR
      STEADFAST LOVE.

Presider: The Lord hears the sound of my weeping;

All: ALL MY ENEMIES SHALL BE ASHAMED
      AND STRUCK WITH TERROR.

Presider: Stir up your might
           and come to save us.

All: RESTORE US, O GOD;
      LET YOUR FACE SHINE,
      THAT WE MAY BE SAVED.

PRAYERS

Holocaust

1   God, just and merciful,
      the same yesterday, today, and tomorrow;
      have mercy upon our humanity in its blindness,
      its bitterness, and its confusion.
      Deliver us, O Lord, from lust for power,
      from envy, apathy, and ill will.
      Restore among us good will and mutual trust.
      Lead us in the ways of justice and honor,
      trust and uprightness,

until we are delivered from the bondage
of hate and fear into the light of love and good will.
Amen.

(From the 1985 Christian Service in Memory of the Holocaust, Toronto
[adapted])

2   Presider: O Creator of all the nations of the world,
who calls all humanity to the worship of your
name:

All: BLESSED ARE YOU, WHO CREATED US IN THE
IMAGE OF YOUR ONENESS.

Presider: Shield of Abraham, faithful Savior of Israel, we
rejoice in the continuing life and witness of
their descendants, daughters and sons of the
covenant:

All: WE THANK YOU FOR ABIDING WITH YOUR
PEOPLE THROUGH ALL AGES, EVER RENEWING
YOUR COVENANT.

Presider: O God of Abraham and Sarah, Isaac and
Rebecca, Jacob, Leah and Rachel, who led your
people of old toward the land of promise:

All: BLESSED ARE YOU, GIVING YOUR PEOPLE THE
GIFT OF NEW LIFE.

Presider: Most High God, awesome God, Creator of all
the living, we stand in awe of your work
among the nations of the world:

All: WE THANK YOU FOR PLANTING YOUR ANCIENT
PEOPLE AT THE CENTER OF THE NATIONS.

Presider: For truths we have learned and have yet to
learn from your revelation to the Israelites,
and treasures we have received and have yet to
receive from the Jewish people today:

All: WE BLESS AND THANK YOU, O LORD.

Presider: That we may learn anew who Jesus was among
his people:

All: WE ASK YOU TO TEACH US, LIVING GOD.

Presider: That we may learn afresh the meaning of Torah
and the Prophets for our lives:

All: WE ASK YOU TO TEACH US, LIVING GOD.

Presider: That we may learn again the understanding you
intend between Christians and Jews:

All: WE ASK YOU TO TEACH US, LIVING GOD.

Presider: For all the hate directed by Christians against
Jews:

All: FORGIVE US, MERCIFUL ONE.

Presider: For teaching that you have abandoned your
ancient people:

All: FORGIVE YOUR CHURCH, MERCIFUL ONE.

Presider: For the continuing inability to receive all your
children in love, wherever it occurs:

All: FORGIVE US, MERCIFUL ONE.

Presider: Rejoicing in the power of the patriarchs,
the cleansing word of the prophets,
the strength of the wisdom teachers,

the devotion of the rabbis,
the courage of the apostles,
the excellence of the martyrs,
and the vitality of the great multitude of
believers in all ages
let us commend ourselves to God.

All: TO YOU, O LORD OUR GOD,
 FOR THE KINGDOM, THE POWER, AND THE
 GLORY ARE YOURS ALONE. AMEN.

(From the 1985 Christian Service in Memory of the Holocaust, Toronto)

3   Mourner's Kaddish

Let the glory of God be extolled.
May God's great name be hallowed,
in a world whose creation God willed.
May God's eternal kingdom soon prevail,
in our own day, our own lives,
and the life of all Israel,
and let us say: Amen.

Let God's great name be blessed
for ever and ever.

Let the name of the Holy One, blessed is God,
be glorified, exalted, and honored,
though God is beyond all the praises,
songs, and adoration that we can utter,
and let us say: Amen.

For us and for all Israel,
may the blessing for peace
and the promise of life come true,
and let us say: Amen.

May God who causes peace to reign in the high heavens,
let peace descend on us,
on all Israel and all the world,
and let us say: Amen.

> (From the 1985 Christian Service in Memory of the Holocaust,
> Toronto. This is substantially the English version found in Gates of
> Prayer [New York: Central Conference of American Rabbis 1975]
> 629-630, adapted for inclusive language by JFH.)

4   El Male Rachmin

O God full of compassion,
Eternal spirit of the Universe,
grant perfect rest under the winds of your Presence
to our loved ones who have entered eternity.
Ruler of Mercy, let them find refuge for ever
in the shadow of your wings,
and let their souls be bound up
in the bond of eternal life.
The eternal God is their inheritance.
May they rest in peace, and let us say: Amen.

> (From the 1985 Christian Service in Memory of the Holocaust,
> Toronto. This is substantially the English version found in
> Gates of Prayer [New York: Central Conference of American
> Rabbis, 1975] 647, adapted for inclusive language by JFH.)

5   Prayer of St Francis

Lord, make us instruments of peace on earth.
Where there is hatred, let us sow love.
Where there is injury, pardon.
Where there is discord, unity.
Where there is doubt, faith.
Where there is error, truth.
Where there is despair, hope.
Where there is sadness, joy.

Where there is darkness, light.
O Divine Ruler, grant that we may not so much seek
To be consoled, as to console,
To be understood, as to understand,
To be loved, as to love.
Amen.

(There are other translations of this prayer. This one is the
version used in the 1985 Christian Service in Memory of the
Holocaust, Toronto)

Hiroshima and Nagasaki

6   God of all creation,
        your dream for humanity is peace, not war.
        Stir up in our memories
        visions of the bombing of Hiroshima and Nagasaki,
        that we may commit ourselves anew
        to the end of nuclear arms
        and the dismantling of all
        weapons of mass destruction.
        This we ask in Jesus' name.
        Amen.

7   God of peace,
        we thank you for progress
        in disarmament, for the destruction of nuclear weapons,
        and for the safer storage and disposal of nuclear waste.
        We thank you as well for the
        beneficial use of radioactivity in medicine and industry.
        Give us wisdom to use the resources of your creation
        only for good, and never in ways that are harmful.
        We ask this in Christ's name.
        Amen.

Creation

8   God of all goodness,
the earth that you created
is torn and disfigured
through human greed,
ignorance and apathy.
Give us the will, the wisdom,
and the gentleness of spirit
to heal and mend our broken earth.
We pray in Jesus' name.
Amen.

9   God our creator,
you have made us an integral part of your creation,
    related to earth and sky, plants and animals,
in the web of your wonderful working.
You also have made us co-creators with you
in building the heavenly city that regains Eden's paradise.
Help us to accept our responsibility for the
healing of creation;
give us wisdom and imagination
and an appreciation of the beauty of your creation.
We pray in Jesus' name.
Amen.

10   By your word,
Lord God,
we and all creatures
are formed, sustained and fed.
Teach us to abide in peace
with the world your hands have made,
that as faithful stewards of your good earth,
we may reverence you in the works of your creation.

We make our prayer through our Lord Jesus Christ,
  your Son,
who lives and reigns with you in the unity of the Holy
Spirit, God forever and ever.

11   Presider: For sky and clouds, for sun, moon and stars:

All: GOD OUR CREATOR, WE THANK YOU.

Presider: For seas and rivers, lakes and streams:

All: GOD OUR CREATOR, WE THANK YOU.

Presider: For the earth and its mountains and hills,
        prairies and deserts:

All: GOD OUR CREATOR, WE THANK YOU.

Presider: For plankton and plants, for trees and flowers:

All: GOD OUR CREATOR, WE THANK YOU.

Presider: For fish and birds, reptiles and mammals:

All: GOD OUR CREATOR, WE THANK YOU.

Presider: For humankind — children, women and men:

All: GOD OUR CREATOR, WE THANK YOU.

Presider: For atoms and galaxies, for everything that is:

All: GOD OUR CREATOR, WE THANK YOU.

Presider: You created this world
        that we might delight in it
        and in it see your handiwork.

We praise you for your goodness,
through Christ our Savior.
Amen.

Violence against Individuals

12   O God,
we look on from a distance,
with Mary Magdalene and the other faithful women,
as Jesus is crucified again in our own day;
Still today your child Jesus cries out,
"My God, my God, why have you forsaken me?"
Still today our brother Jesus is crucified
in our sisters and brothers,
whose clothes are stripped off,
who are mocked and derided,
  beaten and starved.
We weep, and you weep as well:
Your dream for humankind goes awry.
Be with your crucified ones today,
and help us to stand in solidarity with them.
In the name of Jesus Christ.
Amen.

13   Jesus,
Martha and Mary said to you,
"If you had been here,
our brother Lazarus would not have died."
You saw their tears.
You were greatly disturbed in spirit
and deeply moved out of your love for them.
Show your love today,
in this time of distress
and this age of so much death.
Raise up all who suffer violence,

to live in wholeness.
Listen to our prayer
for the sake of your name.
Amen.

14   Presider: Jesus Christ, our brother and liberator,
                    you have told us:
                    Blessed are the poor in spirit,
All: FOR THEIRS IS THE KINGDOM OF HEAVEN.

Presider: Blessed are those who mourn,
All: FOR THEY WILL BE COMFORTED.

Presider: Blessed are the meek,
All: FOR THEY WILL INHERIT THE EARTH.

Presider: Blessed are those who hunger and thirst for
                righteousness,
All: FOR THEY WILL BE FILLED.

Presider: Blessed are the merciful,
All: FOR THEY WILL RECEIVE MERCY.

Presider: Blessed are the pure in heart,
All: FOR THEY WILL SEE GOD.

Presider: Blessed are the peacemakers,
All: FOR THEY WILL BE CALLED CHILDREN OF GOD.

Presider: Blessed are those who are persecuted for
                righteousness' sake,
All: FOR THEIRS IS THE KINGDOM OF HEAVEN.

Presider: Blessed are you when people revile you
and persecute you
and utter all kinds of evil against you falsely
on my account.

All: REJOICE AND BE GLAD,
FOR YOUR REWARD IS GREAT IN HEAVEN.

Presider: We praise you
and we long for the fullness of God's reign.

All: AMEN.

15   *(For victims of abuse)*
O God, in whose enduring love we trust,
bind up the wounds of those betrayed
by abuse at the hands of others.
Heal them and make them whole,
that they may once more receive and give love
with confidence in their dignity as your sons and
daughters.
We ask this through our Lord Jesus Christ, your Son,
who lives and reigns with you in the unity of the
Holy Spirit,
God forever and ever.

> (From original prayers drafted for "Masses for Various Needs and Occasions" by the International Commission on English in the Liturgy. Used with permission. All rights reserved.)

Violence against Groups

16   O God,
today many peoples, nations and groups
hear the shout that Jesus heard:
Crucify them, crucify them.
Today, many are flogged,
stripped of their clothing,

starved, deprived of their homes and lands,
and crucified in many ways.
Be with all who suffer;
weep with them, strengthen them
and hasten the day of justice.
We pray in the name of Jesus Christ.
Amen.

17   Jesus Christ, our savior,
as your boat was being swamped in the storm,
the disciples asked you,
Do you not care that we are perishing?
Today as then, we ask you
to calm the waves, rebuke the wind,
and say, 'Peace!'
We ask you to see our faith,
send us your Spirit,
and preserve us in the hope of your reign.
Amen.

18   O God,
you have promised us that
you will dwell with us as our God,
and that we will be your people;
and one day you will wipe every tear from our eyes,
death will be no more,
and mourning and crying and pain will be no more,
for you make all things new.
We praise you,
and long for the fullness of your reign,
in Jesus Christ's name.
Amen.

19   God ever just,
        you hear the cry of the poor;
        you break the power of the oppressor
        and set the downtrodden free.
        Change inhumanity to compassion
        and let the desires of the affluent
        yield to the needs of the poor.
        Turn our hearts to the way of the gospel,
        that peace may triumph over discord
        and our justice mirror your own.
        Grant this through our Lord Jesus Christ, your Son,
        who lives and reigns with you in the unity of the
        Holy Spirit,
        God forever and ever.

        (From original prayers drafted for "Masses for Various Needs and
        Occasions" by the International Commission on English in the Liturgy.
        Used with permission. All rights reserved.)

20   God of justice,
        you adorned the human race
        with a marvelous diversity,
        yet clothed each of its members
        with a common dignity
        that may never be diminished.
        Put within us respect for that dignity
        and a passion for the rights which flow from it,
        that we may always champion for others
        the justice we would seek for ourselves.
        Grant this through our Lord Jesus Christ, your Son,
        who lives and reigns with you in the unity of the
        Holy Spirit,
        God forever and ever.

        (From original prayers drafted for "Masses for Various Needs and
        Occasions" by the International Commission on English
        in the Liturgy. Used with permission. All rights reserved.)

BLESSINGS

1   May the God of Abraham and Sarah,
of Moses and Miriam,
of Job and Judith,
of Jesus and Mary,
bless us all and be with us always.
Amen.

> (From the 1985 Christian Service in Memory of the Holocaust, Toronto)

2   May the God of creation,
the God of wisdom,
the God of mercy,
bless us and remain with us always.

3   May the God who created the stars,
the sun and the moon,
the earth, seas and sky,
the plants, animals and humankind,
bless us and be with us always.

4   May the God who heals
touch us and our violent world,
and bless us and be with us always.

5   May She who is the strength of our life
lead us to new life.
May He who had courage to condemn inspire us.
And may Love be our constant companion.

> (From Denise Davis Taylor, Edmonton)

COMMISSIONING/DISMISSALS

The presider gives the blessing and the commissioning, and the whole assembly replies "Thanks be to God."

1   Go now and choose love instead of fear,
responsibility instead of indifference.
Go forth to act justly, love tenderly,
and walk humbly with our God.
Go and work for a world
in which the rights of all are guaranteed.

2   Go now to bring peace,
to use creation wisely,
and to care for all sisters and brothers
around the world.

3   Go now to heal creation,
to live as co-creators with God,
to prevent further abuse of creation,
and to see the hand of God in all that is.

4   Go now to heal and convert,
to denounce violence
and to console those who are hurting.
Go and be the hands and heart
of Jesus Christ in our world today.

5   Go now to denounce violence,
to listen to the cries of the violated,
to walk with abusers and the abused,
to live the strength of Christ.

(From Denise Taylor, Edmonton)

11. PRAYERS IN LITURGICAL BOOKS

THE ROMAN CATHOLIC SACRAMENTARY

The sacramentary is the book of prayers for Mass. Although a liturgy of lament may not be the Mass—especially if it is ecumenical or interfaith—the prayers in the sacramentary, particularly the opening prayers and the blessings, may still be used. Consult the section called "Masses and Prayers for Various Needs and Occasions." There you will find prayers organized according to these topics:

> For persecuted Christians
>
> For civic needs: For nation, province/state, or city
>
> For the progress of peoples
>
> For peace and justice
>
> Other prayers for peace
>
> In time of war or civil disturbance
>
> For productive land
>
> Other prayers for productive land
>
> In time of famine or for those who suffer from famine
>
> Prayers to be said by those suffering from hunger
>
> For refugees and exiles
>
> For those unjustly deprived of liberty
>
> For prisoners

In time of earthquake

For rain

For fine weather

To avert storms

For any need

THE BOOK OF BLESSINGS

The 1989 Roman Catholic *Book of Blessings* offers liturgies of the word with prayers of blessing for the following:

Order for the Blessing of a Victim of Crime or Oppression

Order for the Blessing of Animals

Order for the Blessing of Fields and Flocks

Order for the Blessing of Seeds at Planting Time

Order for a Blessing on the Occasion of Thanksgiving
for the Harvest

The version of the *Book of Blessings* for use in households, *Catholic Household Blessings and Prayers*, encourages fasting and prayer (and gives some texts) on the following occasions:

Ember Days, including prayers for August 6 and August 9;

Feast of the Holy Innocents, December 28;

Yom Hashoah (date varies)

LUTHERAN BOOK OF WORSHIP

The 1978 minister's desk edition has a section titled "Petitions, Intercessions, and Thanksgivings," with prayers organized under these topics:

Peace among the nations

Peace

Social justice

The variety of races and cultures

The unemployed

Our enemies

The poor and the neglected

The oppressed

Those who suffer for the sake of conscience

Harvest of lands and waters

Conservation of natural resources

In time of scarce rainfall

Dangers of abundance

Those in affliction

THE BOOK OF COMMON PRAYER

The 1979 worship book of the Episcopal church has a section titled "Prayers and Thanksgivings," with prayers under these topics:

For peace

For peace among the nations

For our enemies

For social justice

In times of conflict

For agriculture

For the unemployed

For the poor and neglected

For the oppressed

For prisons and correctional institutions

For knowledge of God's creation

For the conservation of natural resources

For the harvest of lands and waters

For rain

For the future of the human race

BOOK OF ALTERNATIVE SERVICES

This 1985 worship book of the Anglican church of Canada has a section titled "Occasional Prayers," with prayers under these headings:

For the oppressed in this land

For the unemployed

For the poor and neglected

For our enemies

For prisons and correctional institutions

For those who suffer for the sake of conscience

THE UNITED METHODIST BOOK OF WORSHIP

The 1992 edition has a section, "Special Sundays and Other Special Days," that includes prayers for these occasions:

Human Relations Day

Native American Awareness Sunday

Peace with Justice Sunday

Martin Luther King, Jr. Day

See also the section titled "Prayers for Various Occasions":

For creation

For peace

For safety

In time of natural disaster

For justice

The section titled "Blessings for Persons" offers these prayers:

> For those who suffer
>
> For a victim or survivor of crime or oppression

Several prayers from Native American traditions are in other sections of this book: See numbers 455, 468, 470, 487, 521.

BOOK OF COMMON WORSHIP

The 1993 worship book of the Presbyterian Church (U.S.A.) has prayers for these intentions:

> For peace
>
> For racial peace
>
> For racial and cultural diversity
>
> For peace among nations
>
> For hope
>
> For creation
>
> For fruits of the earth
>
> For the harvest
>
> When there is a natural disaster
>
> For natural resources
>
> For nature
>
> For social justice
>
> For the afflicted
>
> For the oppressed
>
> For the outcast
>
> For the poor and neglected
>
> For those in distress
>
> At a time of tragedy
>
> For the unemployed

12. OTHER PUBLICATIONS

GENERAL

Celebrating One World: A Liturgy Resource Book (London: CAFOD and St. Thomas More Centre, 1987).

Grant Us Peace (Chicago: Liturgy Training Publications, 1991).

With All God's People: The New Ecumenical Prayer Cycle, compiled by John Carden (Geneva: World Council of Churches, 1989).

HOLOCAUST

Gates of Prayer: The New Union Prayerbook (New York: Central Conference of American Rabbis, 1975). Service for Tish'a be-Av and Yom Hashoah on pages 573-589.

Siddur Sim Shalom: A Prayerbook for Shabbat, Festivals, and Weekdays. Ed. Jules Harlow (New York: The Rabbinical Assembly. The United Synagogue of America, 1985). Readings for Yom Hashoah on pages 828-843.

Marcia Sachs Littell. *Liturgies on the Holocaust. An Interfaith Anthology* (Lewiston, New York and Queenston, Ontario: Edwin Mellen Press, 1986).

Eugene J. Fisher and Leon Klenicki. *From Death to Hope: Liturgical Reflections on the Holocaust* (New York: Stimulus Foundation, 1983).

Days of Remembrance: A Department of Defense Guide for Annual Commemorative Observances, 2nd ed. (Washington DC: Office of the Secretary of Defense, 1989).

Shoshana Kalisch with Barbara Meister. *Yes, We Sang! Songs of the Ghettos and Concentration Camps* (San Francisco: Harper & Row, 1985).

NUCLEAR POWER

My People, I Am Your Security: Worship Resources in a Nuclear Age (Washington, D.C.: Sojourners, 1982).

CREATION

Searching for the New Heavens and the New Earth: An Ecumenical Response to UNCED (Geneva: World Council of Church's Group on UNCED, 1992).

Scott McCarthy. *Celebrating the Earth: An Earth-Centered Theology of Worship with Blessings, Prayers, and Rituals* (San Jose: Resource Publications, 1991).

Nellie van Donkersgoed, ed. *Sabbath for the Environment*, 2nd ed. (Guelph Ontario: Jubilee Foundation for Agricultural Research n.d.).

UN *Environmental Sabbath: Earth Rest Day*. (New York: UN Environmental Program, 1990).

WOMEN

Rosemary Radford Ruether. *Women-Church: Theology and Practice of Feminist Liturgical Communities* (San Francisco: Harper & Row, 1986).

Miriam Therese Winter. *Women Prayer Women Song: Resources for Ritual* (Oak Park, Illinois: MeyerStone, 1987).

Miriam Therese Winter. *WomenWord*, 3 vol. (New York: Crossroad, 1990, 1991, 1992).

Family Violence in a Patriarchal Culture (Ottawa: The Church Council on Justice and Corrections and The Canadian Council on social Development, 1988).

NATIVE AMERICANS

Joyce Carlson, ed. *The Journey: Stories and Prayers for the Christian Year from People of the First Nations* (Toronto: Anglican Book Centre, 1991).

Joyce Carlson, ed. *Spirit of Gentleness: Lenten Readings and Prayers* (Toronto: United Church of Canada n.d.).

Paul Steinmetz. *Meditations with Native Americans — Lakota Spirituality* (Santa Fe NM: Bear & Co., 1984).

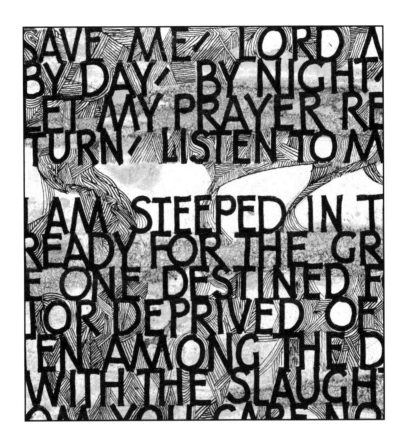

INTERCHURCH (ECUMENICAL) SERVICES

An ecumenical liturgy is one designed to be celebrated by Christians from various churches. Two types of ecumenical service are commonly encountered:

1. A service sponsored and hosted by Roman Catholics, to which guests from other churches are invited. This type of service typically would be planned entirely or mostly by the Roman Catholic host community, though there may be input from others as well. In addition, it probably would be presided over by a Catholic (ordained or lay), and other ministries (such as music, hospitality) probably would be carried out by Catholics. Guests, however, may well be invited to share in such ministries as reading, leading prayers and giving a blessing. Guest clergy may be invited to vest and may be seated prominently. Finally, the structure and content of the service would most likely come from the Roman Catholic tradition, though every attempt should be made to be hospitable and foster the full participation of the guests.

2. An interchurch service, sponsored and hosted by members of more than one church. In this situation, all the Christian communities represented would share in planning and in ministry, and the structure and content would reflect all the participating traditions.

The section that follows contains suggestions and raises questions that will help in the planning and celebration of ecumenical liturgies of either type.

Preparing the Liturgy The following questions need to be considered:

Who will participate in the service: Are only two churches involved, or more? What is the range of backgrounds, experiences, theological views and expectations of the communities involved?

What do the churches involved have in common? Do people know one another, or do they have to be introduced? Have the congregations worked, studied or worshiped together in the past? This will influence the type and extent of liturgical hospitality that is appropriate, as well as what is needed to promote maximum participation.

What is the occasion? This, of course, is a normal question for preparing liturgy.

Where will the liturgy take place? Is it the place of worship of one of the churches involved or some other place? Besides the general space issues discussed earlier (see pages 23 – 24), ecumenical worship raises some other questions: Will the furnishings, imagery, artwork or arrangement of the place be problematic for any of the participants?

How can this service foster Christian unity? This should be a conscious motivation of the planning group and not just assumed.

How can this service be hospitable, with respect to fellowship in general and the prayer of all present? Great care needs to be taken not to ignore the presence or sensitivites of anyone present.

Are there any customs or courtesies that need to be observed? The planning group should check this out.

Will more than one language be used? How can this be done hospitably? This might be relevant if ethnic congregations or Eastern parishes are involved.

How do the churches and clergy involved wish to be named or addressed? Do not assume that what you call a particular church or how you address its clergy is what they prefer to be called; check it out.

Is there anything that might be particularly offensive to any person, group, or church, and thus ought to be avoided?

Structure of the Liturgy Deciding what basic model of liturgy to use will be one of the main responsibilities of the planning group. The churches represented in the planning group may have quite different customary ways of beginning and ending services. Thus, although Roman Catholics are used to a scriptural greeting at the beginning of the eucharist and a verse and response at the beginning of the liturgy of the hours, some other traditions start services with a short passage from scripture read by the minister, with or without congregational response. Likewise, some traditions have a more structured and outward-directed conclusion (dismissal, commission) at the end of the service than is typical of Roman Catholic liturgies. All these practices are valid; choices will have to be made.

Scripture and Preaching Most Christian services will include the proclamation of one or more passages from scripture. Roman Catholics need to remember that Anglicans and Protestants generally do not accept as inspired scripture certain books of the Hebrew Scriptures (the deuterocanonical books).

Other decisions to make include what translation(s) of scripture to use (some churches are more used to one than another) and whether to read from a lectionary or a whole bible (again, different churches prefer one or the other).

The psalms often are used in ecumenical as well as regular services, but the planning group needs to be aware that these are used in different ways by various churches. Some congregations customarily read selections, while others sing or read the entire psalm or at least large sections. The planning group needs to decide not only which psalms will be used in an ecumenical liturgy but how those psalms will be used as well.

Finally, whether or not to use nonscriptural readings will have to be decided upon. Again, this practice is more common in some churches than others, and there is greater freedom to do this in ecumenical services than in the Sunday liturgy.

The proclamation of scripture usually is followed by some kind of reflection on the passages read. Decisions regarding preaching include the style or approach taken (which may vary among churches), length, orientation or theme, the number of preachers, and who they are. In most traditions, preachers are ordained ministers; but in ecumenical services, this need not always be the case.

Silent prayer after the readings and after the preaching makes good sense, but this practice is more common in some traditions than in others.

Prayer Texts The source of spoken prayers might be the service books or traditional liturgical materials of the various churches involved; the prayers might be composed for the occasion; or the prayers might be improvised. While Roman Catholics might be more accustomed to prayers already composed and found in their liturgical books, ministers of some other traditions may prefer to compose their own prayers for the occasion. And ministers of still other churches would be more comfortable improvising them. The planning group cannot take such matters for granted.

Decisions will also have to be made about who will say such verbal prayers: the presiding minister, another minister, the congregation, the minister and congregation in dialogue, or some other individual or group. Different churches are used to different ways of doing this.

Music The choice of music may be dependent on what hymnals are available in the particular church or other location where the worship will take place. Alternatively, other books will have to be obtained or the music to be used will have to be included in a bulletin or some sort of handout. (Of course, copyright permission will be obtained ahead of time for any music that is reprinted.)

Remember that different churches have different musical traditions and that some tend to use responsorial-style singing, while others are more familiar with through-composed music. Some are used to singing harmony, while others use only the melody line.

Who will do the individual music selections: congregation, choir, soloists, cantor and congregation, instrumentalists, and/or others? In particular, the role of the choir differs among churches.

Ministry It is especially appropriate in an ecumenical service that ministry be shared.

One or a small number of persons will have to be chosen to preside over the service. If there is more than one presider, it is most appropriate that they should be from different churches.

Clergy other than those who preside may provide at least visual representation of their churches by being seated appropriately. A decision should be made regarding their vesture; they may wish to wear their customary liturgical garb (if they use any), even though this probably will result in a variety of costumes. Alternatively, they may choose to wear street dress and not be seated in special places.

As already indicated, one or more preachers should be chosen; the preacher may or may not be one of the presiding ministers.

The reading of scripture is another ministry that could be shared. Churches differ regarding whether some or all scripture is read by lay persons or by clergy, and in ecumenical services, freedom on this point is possible. It must be decided ahead of time, however. When possible, readers should represent several of the gathered church communities.

Ministers of hospitality (who have a variety of names in different churches) are especially important in ecumenical services. Again, those chosen should be representative of the different churches that will be gathering.

Finally, the ministers of music are extremely important. Instrumentalists, soloists, choir(s), cantor(s), and leaders of congregational singing all might be needed. If possible, they also should represent different churches, though this is not always practical.

Nonverbal elements A common temptation in liturgy planning of any kind is to make the service too verbal; but texts are only part of the great tradition of Christian worship. The importance of silent prayer has already been mentioned. Other nonverbal elements should also be considered by the planning group (see pages 23 – 24).

In preparing an ecumenical liturgy, certain issues regarding the worship environment and the use of gestures need to be examined from the perspectives of theology and hospitality.

What visual signs and symbols will be prominent: a cross or crucifix, icons, candles, water, or incense? What will be the significance of these things, if any, to the participating churches? Are any of these things likely to be misinterpreted and/or cause offense or distraction?

What kinds of postures and gestures are planned? How comfortable will the members of the participating churches be with these? Roman Catholics are relatively comfortable with a variety of postures and gestures done in unison and requiring very little thought. Orthodox Christians sometimes stand through their entire liturgy, bowing and crossing themselves at certain points. Some Christian churches do not kneel as part of their worship, and others sit a great deal. Some bow, some lift up their arms or wave their hands, and some sway to singing. In some churches these things are defined and practiced in unison, and in other churches postures and gestures are spontaneous or left to the individual. The planning group needs to take all of these variations into account.

Congregational Participation Finally, planners should be sure that the service involves everyone present and not just the ministers (whether clergy or laity). There should be a good balance of "proclamation" (from the front) and "response" (from the pews).

This participation may require printed materials of some kind; bulletins or orders of service of some kind are often used. Planners should be aware that some traditions tend to print all the materials in such bulletins, whether said or sung by ministers, congregation or musicians; others print only texts used by the congregation, plus minimal directions and context.

INTERFAITH SERVICES

An interfaith service is one celebrated by Christians and non-Christians. For many Christians this is a fairly new concept and experience; therefore, it has to be approached with serious thought and careful planning.

Common prayer among people of different faiths presupposes that their traditions have something in common. Prior to the Second Vatican Council, the Roman Catholic church did not feel it had enough in common with non-Christians (in fact, even with other Christians) to permit common prayer with theological integrity. The Council, however, stated quite clearly that there were definite religious values in Judaism, Islam, Hinduism, Buddhism and other world religions, and that these values were recognized and appreciated by the Catholic church. This has been repeatedly emphasized by popes and Vatican offices since that time. Exactly how this commonality is to be understood theologically is still being worked out by theologians, and some Christian churches and schools of theological thought view these developments with grave misgivings.

Though the first large step in interfaith relations has been to recognize significant religious values in non-Christian religions, it is still another large step to move toward common prayer with members of other faiths. This movement has been cautiously encouraged by the Roman Catholic church, especially with respect to Jews and Muslims. More recently, Pope John Paul II has taken part in services of prayer for world peace that have included representatives of many different world religions as well as representatives of many Christian churches.

Common prayer between Christians and non-Christians may not be a regular event in the lives of individuals or local communities. At the present time, at least, it is a special event, occurring at times when extenuating circumstances bring people closer together than usual. Such times might be civic affairs or public school functions, times of social trials (war, nuclear disarmament, civil unrest, discrimination) or natural disasters.

Common prayer should emphasize what the faiths of those groups participating in the liturgy have in common, not what divides them. Thus, there necessarily will be tension between sensitivity to the other faith(s) involved and faithfulness to one's own tradition. Such selectivity is legitimate in liturgy: In no single liturgy, even of one's own church, can everything be said; choices are always being made. So, while the greatest participation of all present is to be fostered and encouraged, deliberate ambiguity, blurred meanings and theological inconsistency are to be avoided.

As with ecumenical services, interfaith services can be of two types: (a) a service sponsored and hosted by Roman Catholics, in which guests from other faiths are involved, or (b) a service sponsored by members or communities of more than one faith.

Scholars and pastoral practitioners have suggested three approaches to preparing interfaith services.

> 1. In the first model, each group in turn does from its tradition what it deems appropriate for the occasion; there may or may not be some common ground, but each group proceeds relatively independently.

> 2. The second model embodies greater structural unity and order in the service, based on preliminary common planning; the service is filled out using traditional prayers and music from each tradition.

> 3. The third model is similar to the second, except that new prayers and materials are prepared for the occasion by representatives of the traditions involved.

Rabbi Lawrence Hoffman takes a somewhat different approach, or at least uses different language in describing some of these possibilities. He distinguishes three types of interfaith services:

> 1. An assembly in which a particular tradition celebrates its own faith in its own way, with guests from another tradition,

is known as an *Indigenous Service with Guests*. The appropriate service is whatever the host religion would normally do, with perhaps the addition of some explanatory mechanism to make the guests feel at home.

2. As assembly in which different religious traditions meet to celebrate or to mark something that members of all the traditions have in common will normally call for a *Service of the Highest Common Denominator*. This will avoid particular references or practices that exclude some members of the assembled gathering.

3. On some occasions when a truly common gathering occurs, it may be desirable and possible to hold a *Service of Mutual Affirmation*. Such services are structured so that the various religious traditions represented are given the opportunity to worship side by side, as it were, alternately speaking in their own particular way and then silently witnessing to their co-worshipers doing the same.

Other important considerations include the place of the service; often a "neutral" location is preferable to the regular place of worship of one of the faiths involved. Silence has also been found to be important, acting as a unitive factor when speech is not so unifying. Finally, simple and commonly appreciated nonverbal elements, such as candles and flowers, are also important.

The most important thing to remember is that what is essential in interfaith worship is great sensitivity to all those involved as well as respect for the integrity of one's own faith.